Original title:
The Search for Meaning in the Cookie Dough

Copyright © 2025 Creative Arts Management OÜ
All rights reserved.

Author: Milo Harrington
ISBN HARDBACK: 978-1-80566-091-0
ISBN PAPERBACK: 978-1-80566-386-7

Chasing Crumbs of Clarity

In the bowl, a swirling mess,
I ponder life, I must confess.
A whisk in hand, I take a stance,
Does this batter hold a chance?

With each scoop, I find a clue,
Eggs and sugar, just like glue.
Searching for answers, I taste my fate,
Is that wisdom, or just dessert plate?

Sweet Ingredients of Existence

Life's a mix of flour and dreams,
Sifting hope, or so it seems.
Piping bags filled with wishes wide,
Sprinkles to share, or just to hide?

I beat the butter, oh so sweet,
Where's the meaning in this treat?
A dash of salt, a pinch of fun,
Did I just bake a life well done?

The Floury Quest

On a quest for truths, sticky and round,
In every swirl, new joys are found.
Cupcake dreams and muffin sighs,
What's beneath the floury skies?

As I roll out the dough, a thought does bloom,
Is joy just icing, or something in the room?
With sugar highs and chocolate lows,
I guess we make do with what we chose.

In the Depths of Chocolate Chip Reverie

In chocolate rivers, I dive so deep,
Whisking away the thoughts I keep.
A cookie castle, grand and tall,
With marshmallow clouds that rarely fall.

Each bite peels back the layers of fun,
Who knew dough could shine like the sun?
In my sweet retreat, I clap my hands,
Life's a cookie, just take your plans.

Kneading Questions

In the bowl, I mix and stir,
Is this life or just a blur?
Butter dreams and sugar sighs,
What's the point in cookie highs?

I knead my doubts, they grow and swell,
Is this heaven or just a shell?
Eggs of hope, vanilla's tease,
Can dough bring me inner peace?

I roll the dough, I can't decide,
Are these cookies meant to hide?
Chocolate chips like dreams deferred,
Crumbled thoughts that go unheard.

With every scoop, I take a chance,
In this dough, I find my dance.
Sprinkles bright, like laughter's call,
Do they mean I've found it all?

A Taste of Purpose

A dash of hope, a sprinkle lie,
What brings joy? A cookie high?
Do these flavors hold the key,
To a life that's full and free?

I bite the cookie, taste the bliss,
Is this sweetness all there is?
In every crumble, answers hide,
Do I have nowhere left to bide?

The oven hums a warm delight,
Are my dreams baked in plain sight?
With every munch, I chew the thought,
Is this the wisdom I have sought?

I dip the dough in silly schemes,
Is it comedy or just dreams?
Floury feet and giggles loud,
I laugh with joy, oh, I'm so proud!

Flour and Fate

A cloud of flour fills the air,
Is life just chaos? Do we care?
Rolling pins of fate collide,
In this kitchen, I confide.

Sugar highs and butter bliss,
Do these crumbs mean something amiss?
With every whisk, I ponder fate,
Can cookies solve the world's debate?

Baking joys and kneaded woe,
I juggle dough, feeling the flow.
Can laughter help the butter rise?
Is there truth behind these pies?

With chocolate chips like hopes to chase,
I smile wide, embrace the space.
Are we all just seeking crumbs?
In the kitchen, joy becomes.

Melting into Thought

As dough begins to melt away,
Do I find truth or just cliché?
Every batch, a merry dance,
In this mess, I take my chance.

Oven preheated, dreams take flight,
Will these cookies shine so bright?
In the mixture, laughter stirs,
In every bite, my heart concurs.

So here I stand, spatula in hand,
Will this cookie help me understand?
With icing dreams and sprinkles bright,
Are these cookies meant for light?

As the timer dings, I cheer,
Is life just baked with love and fear?
I taste the dough, sweet and round,
In this mix, my joy is found.

Ephemeral Delights

In the bowl of life, we stir and sway,
Flour and laughter, come what may,
A sprinkle of joy, a dash of doubt,
What's it all for? Food fights, no doubt!

Chocolate chips dance in gooey fun,
Smoothing out worries, one by one,
But when it's baked, what will we find?
Just crumbs of love, and sugar blind!

The Secrets Beneath Sugar

Underneath the sprinkles, hiding away,
Are the whispered truths of a pastry play,
Eggs and butter, they chatter and gossip,
As the mixer spins, we lose our grip!

Oven timers tick like tiny clocks,
While flour puffs like a friendly box,
What do they know, these treats so sweet?
Maybe life's answers lie in this beat!

Mixing Lives, Molding Dreams

With every scoop, we blend our fates,
Laughter bubbles like batter thick plates,
Rolling pins dance like they're on a spree,
Life's just a recipe, come bake with me!

Mold our hopes like we mold the dough,
Some turn to biscuits, and some, a low blow,
We sprinkle a pinch of wild desire,
And bake it all up in the oven's fire!

Chasing Sweet Epiphanies

I chase the flavor of thoughts so bright,
In doughy dreams that take flight at night,
Sifting wisdom with sugar high,
What's the recipe? Who knows, oh my!

The spatula winks, it stirs my fate,
Each bite of truth is a sugary date,
And when it's gone, alas, we grin,
For in each moment, sweet joys begin!

Essence of the Edible

In a bowl of dreams I find,
The sweetness that feels so aligned.
Chocolate chips, a treasure trove,
In every bite, my spirit's wove.

A pinch of this, a dash of that,
My heart does dance like a playful cat.
With flour clouds and sugar sighs,
My joy unfolds, oh what a prize!

Raw delights, a guilty thrill,
With every scoop, I feel a chill.
But oh, the laughter in my soul,
In edible essence, I feel whole!

A spoonful here, a cheeky taste,
In cookie dough, there's no time to waste.
Life's meaning hides in buttery bliss,
I take a bite and can't resist!

Between the Spoonfuls

Between the spoonfuls, I ponder,
The cosmic joke, I begin to wander.
A dollop of fate, a sprinkle of chance,
In cookie dough, I find my dance.

Eggs and sugar, a blend so fine,
With each mix, I feel divine.
Whisking away my worries and woes,
The dough reveals what nobody knows.

Laughter erupts with each gooey scoop,
In the chaos, I find my loop.
Baking isn't just for the hungry,
It's where my thoughts become so funky!

Oh, the joy of a half-baked dream,
In every bite, life starts to gleam.
Between the spoonfuls and all that's mixed,
I find my purpose, sweetly fixed!

Craving the Unseen

I crave the unseen, the taste of fate,
In each raw morsel, I celebrate.
The universe whispers in chocolate swirls,
With every bite, the chaos unfurls.

Under the counter, secrets lie,
Flour dust and laughter fill the sky.
What's hidden within this sugary mass?
Could it be wisdom, or just some sass?

Rolling dough like a ball of glee,
I find my meaning; it's playful, you see.
In each crumb, there lies a quest,
To bake up joy and be truly blessed!

So grab a spoon, let's make a mess,
Embrace the dough, it's pure happiness.
In cravings' dance and candied spree,
I taste existence, wild and free!

Stirred Sands of Purpose

In stirred sands of purpose, I find my way,
Each grain a memory, come out to play.
Butter and sugar, my guiding light,
In cookie dough's embrace, everything's right.

Sprinkle some laughter, whisk in a smile,
In this tasty journey, let's stay a while.
Baking madness, oh what a thrill,
With every bite, I get my fill.

From mixing bowl to happy sighs,
Finding my truth 'neath sugary skies.
There's joy in the gooey, sweet stuff,
Life's simple pleasures are more than enough!

So as I fold, blend, and create,
In stirring dough, I contemplate.
In every scoop, my zest is clear,
The essence of life, oh so near!

Embracing What Rises

In a bowl of chaos, I mix and I stir,
Cookies are calling, it's a sweet little blur.
Flour clouds dance, making my nose twitch,
Laughter erupts, oh what a fun witch!

Baking soda's a friend, it lifts us so high,
Like dreams in the oven, we reach for the sky.
Chocolate chips tumble, like stars in a night,
I find joy in the mess, oh what a delight!

Rolling in dough, I lose track of time,
Each scoop a giggle, each taste a new rhyme.
Flavors collide, a wild, tasty drama,
It's deeper than cookie, it's life in a panorama!

With every bite taken, I chuckle at fate,
Life's silly recipe, let's bake up some fate!
Sprinkles of happiness, a sprinkle or two,
In this doughy adventure, I find my true crew!

Whisking Away Insecurities

With a whisk in hand, I beat down my doubt,
Eggs and sugar, mix without a pout.
Fluffy intentions, rise up from the bowl,
Each swirl of my batter feeds my hungry soul.

Flour flies high, like my worries take flight,
There's joy in the chaos, oh what a sight!
Melted butter pools, a soft, creamy dream,
The essence of 'me' starts to bubble and beam.

Sprinkling salt, like wisdom anew,
Baking away fears, just me and the brew.
In every dilemma, I fold in some cheer,
A pinch of the past, but no need to fear!

When the timer dings, I'll open the door,
Warm cookies await, couldn't ask for more.
Each morsel a laugh, a friendship so sweet,
Together we conquer—oh, what a treat!

Morsels of Meaning

Doughy delights, each knead tells a tale,
Tasty adventures, I'm setting my sail.
Morsels of joy in a sprinkle of zest,
Finding true treasures in life's tasty quest.

Crumbs of confusion, I mix with some glee,
Adding a dash of purpose, just like my tea.
In the oven of chaos, my dreams start to rise,
Golden aspirations beneath sweetening skies.

Chips of kindness melt into my heart,
A recipe crafted, each ingredient an art.
In the crunch of the cookie, I manage to see,
The laughter of life, it's a recipe!

So let's roll with this dough, sing songs of delight,
For meaning is more than just black or white.
In every sweet moment, I find a new bite,
Together in laughter, everything feels right!

Tasting the Unknowable

In the bowl, a mystery lies,
With chocolate chips and quantum pies.
I dip my spoon, a fearless knight,
Savoring flavors, much to my delight.

What is this dough? Perhaps it's fate,
Or merely snacks from a twist of fate.
I ponder life, with every bite,
Is this dessert my guiding light?

Fingers sticky, laughter fills the air,
Why think too hard? Just grab a chair.
I toss in nuts, a wild guess,
In this sweet chaos, I find success!

No recipe can explain the fun,
In every gooey spoon, the world has spun.
So let's indulge, let's not be shy,
In the cookie dough, our dreams will fly.

Unfolding Ingredients of the Heart

Eggs and flour, a heart's embrace,
In mixing bowls, we find our place.
The sugar swirls like laughter shared,
With every stir, my worries bared.

A dash of salt, a pinch of glee,
Could this blend define 'me'?
With every scoop, I take a chance,
In this doughy dance, I find romance.

I add some sprinkles, colors bright,
Like hopes and dreams through darkest night.
What's hidden here? A whimsy quest,
In creamy textures, I feel so blessed.

But wait! The timer's ticked away,
Will it rise or just decay?
Open the oven, oh what a sight!
In cookie form, my dreams take flight!

Brushing Against the Infinite

With flour clouds and giggles near,
I brush the dough, no room for fear.
What comes next? I dare to dream,
In sticky fingers, I find my scheme.

A swirl of butter, a pinch of fun,
Mixing memories till the day is done.
Is life this dough, a rolling spree?
To savor each moment, just like a cookie.

I toss in whims, a dash of cheer,
Through crispy edges, my path is clear.
Oh, what wisdom in crumbs I find,
Life's sugary chaos is well-defined.

So grab a spoon and join the ride,
In every nibble, let joy abide.
In this absurdity, we'll surely thrive,
With cookie dough, we feel alive!

Sugar-Coated Insights

A sprinkle here, what could it mean?
Life's just sugar, sweet and keen.
I mix my hopes with chocolate chips,
In this treat, wisdom freely slips.

Each scoop's a chance, a new delight,
With laughter echoing in the night.
What tricks can we bake, what joys to find?
In every cookie, the universe aligned.

Frosting thoughts swirl, colors collide,
These decadent musings, I won't hide.
The spatula twirls, my spirit takes flight,
This doughy journey feels so right!

So let's not ponder too deeply, my friend,
Just bake it with humor, until the end.
In cookie dough's embrace, we play and sing,
Sugar-coated truths are the best of things!

A Pinch of Philosophy

In a bowl, I ponder fate,
Flour clouds my clueless state.
Eggs and sugar mix and swirl,
What is life? A doughy whirl.

Embracing the Doughy Maze

Rolling pins and dreams collide,
Chocolate chips like stars, they glide.
Twisting paths of sweet embrace,
Is this love or just a taste?

Epiphanies Between Bites

In the oven, truth expands,
Softened hopes in cookie hands.
Chewy insights melt away,
Doughy wisdom on display.

The Crumble of Exploration

Crumbly clues are strewn about,
In each bite, the giggles shout.
Flavors dance and crinkle smiles,
Philosophy's in cookie miles.

Unraveled Sweetness

In a bowl, dreams swirl and toss,
Flour fights back, but who is the boss?
Chocolate chips, like stars, collide,
Finding answers where flavors hide.

A sprinkle of salt, a touch of flair,
Laughter bubbles up in the air.
Roll it, fold it, what comes next?
Baking's just life, a funny text!

Eggs unite, they crack and laugh,
Mix it all up, a joy-filled path.
Spoons like wands, casting sweet spells,
In cookie dough tales, who knows what sells?

The oven hums, secrets confined,
In golden crusts, the answers unwind.
A bite reveals each silly clue,
In a world of dough, it's me and you!

Recipes for the Soul

What's in a bowl? A soul's delight,
Flour and sugar, a whimsical fight.
Mix the oddities, stir up the zest,
Each ingredient, a curious quest.

Eggs waltz around like they own the place,
Butter melts down with a warm embrace.
They giggle and jive, creating a stir,
In this kitchen dance, we all concur.

Vanilla scents the air, dreams take flight,
While spoons sing out, 'Oh, what a sight!'
Sprinklings of laughter in every bite,
Baking our answers, oh what a height!

With each dollop of dough, we'll find our way,
In the chaos of baking, we laugh and play.
Each cookie a story, each batch a cheer,
In the heart of the dough, wisdom is near!

The Bake of Being

Tick-tock goes the oven, what's your plan?
Whisk it all up, be the man!
Cookies in waiting, all gooey and sweet,
Life's like a mix, so stir up that beat!

Baking soda jumps, a fizzy delight,
Flavors collide in a twinkling sight.
Peanut butter hugs chocolate so tight,
In this culinary tale, all feels right.

Rolling out dough, laughter takes flight,
Cutting out shapes, it's quite the sight!
Frosting like dreams, all colorful and bright,
Who knew baking could be so light?

Oh, the joy found in every drop,
Savor each moment, don't ever stop.
Giggling with flour stuck on your face,
In life's sweet kitchen, we find our place!

Tasting Time's Delights

In a whirl of chaos, we find our glee,
Dough on the counter, who's in with me?
Chocolate rivers flow, sugar rains down,
What a strange kingdom, where sweets wear a crown!

Peeking at trays while they cool and chill,
Anticipation grows; oh what a thrill!
Sprinkles like confetti dance 'round my head,
Only in cookie land, can you laugh while you're fed!

With friends by my side, we bake and we bond,
Each taste a reminder of which way we're fond.
A sprinkle of chaos, a dash of a dream,
In these warm treats, life's sweetened theme.

So raise up your spatula, let's give a cheer,
For the flavor adventures that bring us near.
In every dough scoop, joy's delivered right,
Tasting all the delights, oh what a sight!

Rolling Pins and Reveries

In the kitchen we gather, with flour in flight,
Rolling pins dance, oh what a delight!
We laugh and we giggle at each little mess,
Who knew dough could lead to such happiness?

A dash of this, a sprinkle of fun,
Chasing the dreams 'til the baking is done.
We sculpt silly shapes that make no sense,
Muffin tops giggle, it's pure recompense!

With dough on our hands and joy in our hearts,
Each swirl and each roll, a newfound art.
They never quite rise, our creations so bold,
But the stories they tell are worth more than gold!

In this chaotic realm of sweet little treats,
We find life's wonders in sugary feats.
So here's to the laughter, the fun, and the dough,
In this world of delights, let the good times flow!

Sculpting Moments in Sweetness

With floury fingers, I mold and I shape,
A cookie monster, in marvelous cape!
Faces and critters, all in a row,
What's next? A giraffe? Or a friendly hippo?

We giggle and chuckle at absurdity's sight,
As the dough giggles back with sheer delight.
Sprinkles like stars on our artisanal mess,
Who needs perfection? It's joy we possess!

Melty chocolate hugs each creation we make,
Strategic placement for the art's own sake.
No need for a canvas when dough's in my hands,
I paint with my heart; it's the best of all plans!

So let's sculpt our moments, let laughter abound,
In this world of sweetness, pure joy is found.
As ovens await what we craft with such glee,
We bake up some chaos, just you wait and see!

Beyond the Chocolate Chips

Underneath the cocoa and sprinkles, we dive,
In doughy adventures, we're fully alive!
Flavors collide, and we giggle with glee,
Who knew cookie dough could be so carefree?

With every fold, a mystery unfurls,
Beneath all that sugar, hidden joy swirls.
Dough balls become dreams waiting to rise,
Where humor meets sweetness, oh, what a surprise!

So we plop chocolate chips into our fate,
With each little nibble, we celebrate.
The laughter is rising, it's baking divine,
In this funny dough world, oh, how we shine!

With frosting like rainbows, and sprinkles to boot,
In our doughy utopia, we're absolutely cute.
So may our concoctions be wobbly and sweet,
In the cookie dough cosmos, we find life's treat!

Unbaked Aspirations

In bowls of adventure, we dream and we swirl,
Dough in our hands, we give it a whirl.
With visions of cookies so scrumptiously round,
We laugh at the mishaps that know no bounds!

A pinch of ambition, a spoonful of doubt,
Can we make dough rise, without leaving it out?
We ponder the science of flour and cream,
As we occasionally drift off into dream.

With every soft scoop, our hopes redefine,
In the warmth of the kitchen, our spirits align.
Maybe it's gooey, or maybe it's flat,
But the joy in the failures? Just imagine that!

So let's bake up the laughter, let's frolic and play,
In this world of sweet chaos, our hearts lead the way.
Unbaked aspirations, our whimsical dough,
In this tasty adventure, let positivity grow!

Earthy Delights and Universal Questions

In bowls of brown, I ponder wide,
What lies within this gooey tide?
Chocolate chips like stars at night,
Do they have dreams? Oh, what a sight!

Scoop after scoop, my mind takes flight,
Is dough a path to pure delight?
Flour whispers tales, so sweet, so grand,
Do they know secrets? I must withstand!

Eggs and sugar, a curious pair,
Can a cookie teach me how to care?
Cinnamon twirls like a dancer bold,
Sharing stories that never grow old.

As I devour this soft embrace,
I wonder if joy has a face—
Could sprinkles be wise, in silence, wait,
To give laughter to the hungry plate?

Reflections in Sugar and Spice

Stirring thoughts like buttery swirls,
What if desserts could share their pearls?
A dash of nutmeg, a sprinkle of fun,
Is sugar the reason we dance under the sun?

Rolling dough like life's endless quest,
Is it the journey that brings the zest?
With each little bite, I ponder anew,
Do cookies know things we wish we knew?

Laughter echoes from kitchen walls,
Is joy in the batter, or in the brawls?
While munching chips, I must confess,
I'm but a crumb in this sugary mess.

Perhaps the dough holds secrets dear,
Like answering why we gather here—
Maybe the laughter, while we bake,
Explains the meaning in each doughy flake.

Whisked Away by Wonder

With a whisk in hand, I start to dream,
In a bowl of dough, what might I glean?
Could cookie crumbs reveal the past?
Or just a snack, if I ate too fast?

As I measure and mix, the thoughts arise,
What's hidden beneath this sweet disguise?
If flour was wisdom, and sugar was grace,
Could I find answers in every space?

The oven hums a curious tune,
Can cookies hold wisdom under the moon?
As I taste gingerbread's spicy flare,
Do they offer insights, hidden with care?

At the end of this flavorful ride,
Joy's not in answers, but laughs multiplied—
In every bite, the magic's clear,
Life's sweetest lessons are far and near.

The Art of Confectionery Queries

In this doughy quest, I find my way,
Are cookies wise? What do they say?
Sprinkled laughter in every bite,
Could frosting really be pure delight?

Creaming butter, thoughts start to swirl,
What mysteries lie in each doughy whirl?
The oven's warmth, a gentle embrace,
Could this be life's whimsical race?

Perhaps the oats share tales of yore,
While sugar giggles and asks for more—
When chocolate chunks clink, do they conspire,
To share their secrets, set hearts on fire?

So here I stand with a spatula wide,
Creating wonders, letting joy slide—
In every crumb, there's laughter, you see,
For cookies are more than just dough to me!

Ingredients of Identity

In flour's embrace, we find our way,
A pinch of salt keeps doubts at bay.
Baking soda's rise takes us high,
While sugar sprinkles sweeten the sigh.

Eggs beat out our fears with flair,
Together, mixed, we dare to share.
Each ingredient blends our tale so bold,
Through doughy dreams, our fate unfolds.

Chocolate chips, those little stars,
Guide our quest near and far.
In every scoop, a story spins,
A recipe crafted where each heart wins.

So roll and knead, let laughter flow,
In this big bowl of life, we glow.
Each bite a bubble of joy divine,
In every crumb, our lives align.

Rolling Through Revelations

Rolling pins and laughter blend,
With every thud, our worries end.
Dough rolls out, so soft and warm,
Creating chaos—a yummy storm.

Flipping spatulas with glee,
Surprises hide in every spree.
Genie in a cookie jar,
Pulls out secrets from afar.

Sprinkled joy on every batch,
Life's riddles solved with a tasty match.
Chocolate swirls reveal the plot,
In each gooey mess, we find a lot.

Tomorrow's treats become today's laugh,
Finding flavor in the aftermath.
With flour on our faces, we know it's true,
Each doughy moment brings something new.

Hidden Flavors of Fulfillment

Yummy secrets in every scoop,
Baking dreams with a giggly group.
Ovens crackle, the timer dings,
In warm aroma, laughter sings.

Doughnut holes for hiding fears,
Filling life with joyful cheers.
Sprinkles dance like happy hearts,
A mix of flavors, love imparts.

Ah, the frosting—such sweet delight!
Lipsticky kisses in the night.
With starlit crumbs on our brow,
We nibble truth, and we know how.

So dip your hands in the blissful quest,
In batter thick, we find our nest.
Each scoop a giggle, each taste a spark,
In this doughy dance, we leave our mark.

A Savory Search in Softness

Beneath the surface, flavors tease,
A pinch of fun brings us to our knees.
In this soft dough, we roll our fate,
Laughter baked on our dinner plate.

Cracking eggs like silly jokes,
Flipping spoons with playful pokes.
The gentle warmth of the oven's breath,
A cozy hug that conquers death.

With every fold, the truth unfurls,
A sprinkle of joy in furry swirls.
Life's confections, thick or thin,
In cookie adventures, we begin.

So take a bite, release the cheer,
In this round of dough, bring friends near.
With each delicious, gooey chance,
We mix and mingle, slathered in romance.

Spatula Stories of Life

In the bowl, dreams collide,
Sugar sprinkles, a wild ride.
Flour fluffs like clouds above,
Mixing chaos, oh so much love.

Eggs drop like hopes on the floor,
Spatulas wielded, never a bore.
Choco chips twinkle, a sweet tease,
Whisking away worries with ease.

Spoons dive deep in gooey delight,
Bite-sized wonders, a fun-filled bite.
Crispy edges, doughy centers,
Life's little treasures, our minds enter.

Laughter erupts, flour in the air,
Each scoop a story, a tasty affair.
With every fold, life's woes retire,
Cookie courage fuels our fire.

The Cookie Conundrum

What's the secret? Just pondering,
Baking science, my brain wandering.
Ovens preheat, the clock is set,
Melted butter, a rising threat.

Chocolate chips, where do they hide?
In the dough, like dreams untied.
Rolling pins dance with glee,
Who knew dough held such mystery?

Sprinkle some salt, just for flair,
A pinch of madness, everywhere.
Twists and turns in every batch,
What's the recipe? I'll never catch.

Laughter erupts with each failed try,
Cookies crisp, while hopes fly high.
Though the count might not reveal,
Every bite's got a funny feel.

Between the Grit and the Gloss

In the kitchen, laughter spills,
Cookie sheets give daily thrills.
Between the grit of flour flown,
And glossy dreams of treats well-known.

A dash of sugar, a sprinkle of cheer,
Crumbs on the floor, but no fear here.
Whisk away blues with a gentle hand,
Each swirl of dough, life is unplanned.

Oh, the tales from an oven's heat,
Crispy edges, a comfort sweet.
Between the bites of gooey bliss,
Is life's recipe written in this?

Chase the flavors, chase the fun,
With spatula battles, we're never done.
For in each scoop, laughter is found,
In every swirl, life spins around.

Cravings of the Heart

The oven warms like a summer's day,
Baking dreams in a playful way.
Sifting through thoughts, a sweet mix,
Life's little puzzles, made from quick fix.

Butter's melting, hearts beat fast,
Cookie cravings that forever last.
Rolling dough with laughter's sound,
Joy in each nibble, love's profound.

Crispy bites and giggles blend,
In baking chaos, rules bend.
With every nibble, stories unfold,
Life's chewy moments, a treasure gold.

Frosting dreams, we delve right in,
With sprinkles on top, let the fun begin.
For in each cookie, a little spark,
A sweet reminder to leave a mark.

The Recipe of Existence

In a bowl of flour, dreams collide,
Butter whispers secrets, oh so wide.
Sugar giggles, sweetness afloat,
Eggs crack open, like thoughts remote.

Mix in some chaos, stir a short while,
A dash of laughter, and a goofy smile.
Bake it up quickly, let time take a spin,
Life's just a cookie dough, come on, dive in!

Sprinkles of joy, add a touch of flair,
Tasting the moments, flavors to share.
From lumps of uncertainty, cookies emerge,
Embracing the mess, we happily surge.

With every bite, let our worries unfurl,
Finding contentment in this doughy swirl.
So grab your spoon, let's craft with delight,
In this yummy existence, everything feels right.

Between Spoonfuls and Silence

Between spoonfuls, life stirs in glee,
Mixing the chaos, a tale from me.
Chocolate chips dancing, in perfect sync,
A recipe written in buttery ink.

Tasted the failures, tasted the wins,
Dough on my hands, it's where the fun begins.
Silence is golden, yet cookies do talk,
Whispers of sweetness, as we all flock.

A sprinkle of chuckles, a pinch of cheer,
Even the burnt bits have stories here.
Between the bites and the mischievous grins,
Life's baked in the oven, where humor spins.

So roll up the sleeves, and let's bake anew,
A kitchen of laughter, our dreams to pursue.
With each little spoonful, we conquer the doubt,
In the heart of the dough, joy's what it's about.

Churned Reflections

Swirls of thoughts, like cream in a churn,
Kneading the fabric of life's great turn.
Doughy dilemmas, they rise and they fall,
In the oven of moments, we've got it all.

Rolling the laughter, cutting the strife,
In every cookie, a nibble of life.
Whipping up dreams until they take flight,
We bake with a grin, all through the night.

Yummy and mindless, the batter we make,
Between bites of wisdom, we bake our own fate.
With spatulas ready, let's flip it around,
In the churn of existence, happiness found.

So taste the reflections, the sweetness inside,
Life's just a cookie sheet, let's take it in stride.
With flour on our faces, we chuckle and cheer,
In the kitchen of living, there's nothing to fear.

The Flavor of Foresight

Baking up plans, with a dash of foresight,
Each scoop of joy, making everything right.
Lumps of potential, we roll into dreams,
Life's a big bowl, with laughter in streams.

Craving adventures with chocolate galore,
In every existence, there's always much more.
Sprinkling wisdom on top of the mess,
Finding the flavor in chaos and stress.

A pinch of absurdity, a cup of the strange,
Life's cookie dough will often rearrange.
Bake it all together, then enjoy the show,
In the taste of tomorrow, let happiness grow.

So scoop up your dough, bake it with flair,
Life is much sweeter when we choose to share.
With warmer connections, life's easy and bright,
In the cookie of fate, we find pure delight.

Cracking Open the Cosmos

In a bowl where dreams reside,
Chocolate chips, a cosmic guide.
Flour swirls like stars at night,
With every scoop, the dough takes flight.

Sifting truths through powdered air,
Each bite a question, sweet and rare.
Laughter rises, frothy and light,
As we bake away the cosmic fright.

Mix it up, let flavors blend,
In this dough, we discern and mend.
Sprinkles of wisdom, just a dash,
Life's grand plan, a sugary splash.

When the oven's warmth greets the dough,
A universe of flavors to bestow.
Forks in hand, we dive right in,
Finding joy where the crumbs begin.

The Essence of Everyday Indulgence

A pinch of this, a spoonful that,
Stirring chaos with a spatula spat.
Cookie dough whispers to the heart,
In every bite, a work of art.

Midnight munchies call my name,
Sweet surrender in this doughy game.
Eggs and sugar, a secret pact,
In this treat, I find my act.

Laughter spills like melted cream,
In the kitchen, it's all a dream.
Baking fails and frosted flakes,
Life's a dance; just see what it makes!

When the timer dings, I squeal with glee,
Each cookie a glimpse at giddy me.
With frosted joy, I take a chance,
In every bite, I find my dance.

Whispers in a Whisk

Whisking secrets, oh so sly,
Bubbles burst as giggles fly.
Batter speaks in muffled tones,
Doughy wisdom carved in scones.

In the realm of eggs and cream,
Every swirl a silly theme.
Rolling pins take on a life,
Joking 'round with doughy strife.

Choco-chunks fall like shooting stars,
Marshmallow fluff, a journey far.
Between the mixing and the bake,
Sweet revelations we all make.

Tasting joy with every scoop,
Life's a mixer; let's regroup!
In cookie dreams, we find our way,
To laughter baked, a bright buffet.

Doughy Dreams of Insight

In a mixing bowl, I ponder still,
What flavor brings the biggest thrill?
Nutty wonders swirl about,
With every bite, I laugh and shout.

Rolling out the thoughts I keep,
Baking escapades, oh so deep.
Morsels of hope, an apron's clue,
In doughy depths, I find what's true.

Underneath the oven's light,
Golden edges shining bright.
Each crisp golden rule I learn,
A doughy truth, a silly turn.

So grab a scoop, it's time to bake,
In cookie dreams, let's live awake.
With smeared hands and cheerful cheers,
We'll bake our hopes and quell our fears.

Unbaked Truths

In a bowl of chaos, I mix my fate,
A sprinkle of laughter, it's never too late.
Chocolate chips whisper, secrets in sweet,
Promises of joy, a delicious treat.

Eggs crack with courage, yolks bright as day,
Flour clouds dreams in a frothy ballet.
The world outside spins, but I find my ground,
In gooey concoctions, true bliss can be found.

Rolling Pin Reflections

With a rolling pin wielded, I conquer my doubt,
Flattening worries, letting giggles shout.
Life's like dough, a little messy and wild,
But oh, how it's crafted, the heart of a child.

I knead my ambitions, softening time,
Each roll a reminder, I'll be just fine.
Sugar and spice dance in floury dreams,
Together we rise, or so it seems.

Metaphors Mixed with Milk

Milk swirls like wisdom, creamy and bright,
A splash of absurdity adds to the light.
Mix in some giggles, let seriousness fade,
Each scoop of delight is carefully laid.

When a spoon stirs laughter, it's hard to ignore,
Life's recipe blooms, as we mix and explore.
Measuring joy in cups, a dash of bizarre,
In the kitchen of life, we're all shining stars.

Beyond the Oven's Glow

Beyond the oven's glow, dreams start to rise,
Cookies of whimsy, a wonderful guise.
Behold the aroma, it dances and twirls,
Sprinkles of laughter, a party of swirls.

In a world of delights, I bake with a grin,
Cravings for fun are the best place to begin.
Each bite holds a story, a chance to be free,
In the warmth of the kitchen, it's just you and me.

Doughy Dilemmas

In a bowl so big and round,
I ponder what I've newly found.
Chocolate chips or nuts galore,
Which one do I truly adore?

Whisking fast, I hear a yell,
"Stop! That cookie's doing swell!"
But the dough just laughs and spins,
As I toss in my whims like wins.

Sprinkles rain like confetti bright,
I mix them in with sheer delight.
But will it bake, or will it flop?
Oh, let the sweet confusion pop!

With each scoop, my giggles grow,
Is it dessert, or is it dough?
In this chaos, glee I seek,
Make doughy decisions, oh so cheek!

Sifting through Selves

A pinch of doubt, a scoop of cheer,
In this mixture, who am I here?
Sifting through flour, I find my core,
But crumbs remind me there's always more.

Ingredient labels make me think,
Am I the sugar or the stink?
With every fold, I laugh and sigh,
Am I the cookie, or just the pie?

Baking powder lifts my mood high,
Yet, here I am asking 'why?'
Churning thoughts like dough in a bowl,
What's the recipe to my soul?

As ovens warm, I feel the heat,
Am I the tasty, or just the sweet?
In this kitchen of my head,
Half-baked musings swirl instead!

Oven's Warm Embrace

In the oven's warm embrace,
I question life's ridiculous race.
Are cookies wise, or just there to eat?
With jokes and jests, it's quite a feat!

The timer dings, my heart skips a beat,
Do I want cookies, or just retreat?
Doughy forms perched on the pan,
Planning world domination, what a plan!

But what if I bake my worries in?
Watch calamities turn into a grin?
With every rise, my spirits soar,
In the oven's warmth, I want more!

So bring on life, and all its quirks,
Like sprinkles dancing, it always works,
With each sweet batch, a laugh I'll take,
Embracing chaos, I'll joyfully bake!

Forkfuls of Insight

With fork in hand, I take a dive,
What's beneath this doughy vibe?
A scoop of laughter, a dash of fun,
Bite by bite, I come undone.

Do cookies hold the answers true?
Or is it just the chocolate goo?
Each forkful sends me into bliss,
Sweet revelations, I can't miss!

Looking deeper, I see the truth,
In gooey dough, I find my youth.
Crumbles of wisdom stir the mix,
In every bite, a new comedy fix!

So let's embrace the cookie craze,
Mix and munch through all the maze.
With forkfuls taken, I will claim,
Life's a dessert, not just a game!

Sweet Wisdom in Silhouette

In a bowl of chaos, I stir my fate,
Cocoa whispers secrets, oh so great.
Flour flutters down like life's wild dance,
A sprinkle of sugar, perhaps a chance.

Rolling pins spin tales of doughy delight,
In the kitchen shadows, I ponder at night.
Choco chips glimmer like stars above,
Each bite a riddle, a taste of love.

Baking timers tick, like life's fleeting tune,
Each cookie's a puzzle, revealed by the moon.
Mixing my laughter with some sweet cream,
Finding deep truths in a sugary dream.

With each warm batch, wisdom grows bold,
In crispy edges, mysteries unfold.
Life's a cookie, baked, crumbled, and chewy,
Savor the journey, it's all kind of gooey.

Buttered Dreams and Battered Thoughts

Butter whispers softly as it warms the room,
Dreams blend with sugar, whirling away gloom.
In the mixing madness, thoughts collide,
Flour flies high, like a rollercoaster ride.

Battered minds swirl like the dough in my hands,
Rolling through life's ups, oh where it all lands.
Eggs crack the surface of my weary dreams,
Shiny and yolky, bursting at the seams.

Sprinkling hope over a baking tray,
Like laughter, it rises, come what may.
Chasing the crumbs of a whimsical fate,
In cookie-filled corners, we contemplate.

With each toast of butter, I cling to the fun,
Finding the meaning just barely begun.
In batter and bliss, together we play,
Life's sweet concoction, the chewier the way.

Kneaded Reflections

In the doughy depths, I press out my fears,
Kneading the moments, through laughter and tears.
With every fold, wisdom rises like bread,
A recipe mingled with thoughts in my head.

Rolling my burdens, flattening strife,
Tossing in chocolate, sweetening life.
In a knead for connection, the flavors unite,
Finding fond meanings in each cookie bite.

My spatula dances, swirls bright and bold,
Whisking the tales of the young and the old.
Sprinkle some joy, like snowflakes on top,
With a giggle and smile, my worries just drop.

Each cookie a story, baked warm in the sun,
Frosted reflections, oh what silly fun!
In floury fortunes, I give them a whirl,
Life's punchline in crumbs, as dreams start to twirl.

Crusts of Curiosity

Crusty edges hold wonders, baked with surprise,
Each cookie's a journey, a feast for the eyes.
Beneath the golden tops, curiosity breeds,
Flavorful answers found in our needs.

In a pan of chaotic, sugary dreams,
I dip into questions, unravel it seems.
With each bite I take, my laughter explodes,
Doughy adventures on whimsical roads.

Spritz of the oven, a whiff of delight,
My cravings for meaning, come join in the fight.
With crumbs on my cheek, I ponder anew,
A chuckle, a smile, as flavors break through.

Crusts shaped by stories, the laughter we share,
In cookie-filled moments, I wander without care.
Together we nibble on life's brittle crust,
Finding our purpose, a sweet, silly must.

Layers of Uncertainty

In the bowl where dreams take flight,
Mysterious lumps dance in the light.
I probe with a spoon, a cautious shake,
Is this cookie magic, or a big mistake?

Licking my fingers feels quite divine,
But what's lurking here? Is it sweet or brine?
Chocolate chips giggle, then start to melt,
What's truth in this dough? I've truly felt.

Each scoop a riddle, each taste a clue,
Am I baking cookies or a laundry shoe?
Sprinkles of laughter, a sprinkle of joy,
Doughy debates, my inner chubby boy!

As I ponder the fate of this buttery fate,
I wonder if baked goods appreciate weight.
With a pinch of chaos and a dash of brave,
At the heart of it all, a doughy wave.

Dough-Flavored Discoveries

Rolling the dough with a fabled grin,
Adventures await in the chaos within.
Baking disasters or sugary dreams?
I knead my way through chocolatey schemes.

A sprinkle of joy, a dash of fright,
Should I add the nuts? Oh, what a plight!
Once a simple dough ball, now a quest,
What flavor to find? I ponder and jest.

The cookie crumbs whisper, secrets to share,
Maybe they know where the best sweets are rare.
Should I follow the crumbs or let them go free?
In the realm of the dough, I am truly me!

Stirring the future with a giggle and spin,
What's hidden inside? Will I lose or will win?
Creating a masterpiece, each bite a surprise,
In this floury world, are we wise or just fries?

Unfolding the Whisked Life

With a whisk in hand, I take to the stage,
Fluffy ambitions, I'm turning the page.
Eggs crack open, a yolk full of dreams,
Whisking my troubles, or so it seems.

Sugar swirls in a cloud of bliss,
Will it all end up in a gooey abyss?
The oven hums a sweet lullaby,
As I play the role of the doughy pie guy.

A pinch of this, a dash of that,
Who knew flour could wear a party hat?
Baking my troubles away with a grin,
In this whisked-up life, I only begin!

Recipes whisper, but are they sincere?
The oven beeps, a moment to cheer!
With laughter and chaos, I roll out the dough,
In this whisked life, I'm the star of the show!

Savoring Solitude

In the kitchen's quiet embrace, I stand,
A solitary journey, a spatula in hand.
With cookie dough's charm, I start to adore,
Each bite is a treasure, I can't ignore.

Silently mixing, no judgmental glares,
Just flour and laughter and fond cookie flares.
My oven's a friend, though it doesn't speak,
It warms up my heart, even if I'm meek.

Rolling the dough, I twist and I turn,
Solitude's sweetness, in silence I learn.
What secrets lie deep in this buttery blend?
In moments of quiet, I find a new friend.

With each little scoop, my worries dissolve,
In the world of cookie, my heart will evolve.
So I savor this solitude, rich and profound,
In the dough of my dreams, true joy can be found.

Flour Power: Discoveries in the Mix

In the bowl, all hope is stirred,
A sprinkle here, a dash, unheard.
Baking dreams rise high and tall,
But sometimes they just flop and fall.

Chocolate chips wink slyly bright,
Whisking through the dough feels right.
Flour clouds dance in the air,
Who knew baking could be a dare?

Lumpy lumps tell tales of bliss,
Somewhere hiding a sugary kiss.
With each scoop, a giggle found,
In every bite, joy knows no bounds.

Oven timers beep with glee,
Pans cling to sweet memories.
But really, are we just a mess?
Or is this our doughy success?

The Elixir of Existence

Mixing dreams with cocoa dust,
Beneath the chaos, there's a crust.
A recipe for life's delight,
In every swirl, we take flight.

Eggs crack open, secrets spill,
As laughter rises, we've had our fill.
Who knew this dough could empower?
A midnight snack becomes the hour!

Vanilla whispers sweet and sly,
Reminding us we all must try.
With spoons in hand, we venture wide,
Through doughy paths, we cannot hide.

One more taste, we chant and cheer,
Life's essence is always near.
In cookie dough, we find the spark,
And silly giggles in the dark.

In Pursuit of a Delicious Truth

Rolling pins in the workplace roll,
Searching for that chocolate goal.
Each scoop's a treasure map we trace,
In flour we find our happy place.

Butter glistens like a dream,
In this kitchen, we all scream!
A pinch of hope, a whole lot of fun,
Stirring together till victory's won.

Sprinkle laughter, sugar joy,
Every bite's a favored ploy.
Oven doors promise what's to come,
With every rise, hear the drum!

Underneath the doughy mess,
There lies a truth that's hard to guess.
In each cookie, we taste our quest,
For happiness, our sweetest test.

Sweetness in Solitude

Alone with dough, the world retreats,
In sticky hands, I find my beats.
Chips scattered like stars on high,
In this kitchen, I soar and fly.

Mixing thoughts with floury bliss,
Every swirl, a soft embrace.
Lost in sweetness, giggles bloom,
Dough embraces my quiet room.

Rolling out the doubts of day,
In between, I laugh and play.
A solo dance with spatula strong,
In cookie dough, I truly belong.

As the oven warms, so do I,
With each puff, I almost fly.
A batch of joy, my heart's delight,
In solitude, everything feels right.

Life's Recipe for Joy

In a bowl, we dream and stir,
Sugar's sweet, but life's a blur.
Sprinkle laughter, add a dash,
Bake it slow, enjoy the splash.

Eggs are cracked, like silly jokes,
Flour flies, oh how it chokes!
Chocolate chunks are life's delight,
Taste your troubles, they'll take flight.

Rolling dough, we shape our fate,
Cut out worries, don't be late.
Mix it well, don't overdo,
Every bite brings something new.

With each cookie, joy will rise,
Find the fun in all the pies.
Life's a treat, let's bake some more,
Crumbs of laughter on the floor.

The Undercurrents of Butter

Butter whispers, soft and sly,
Melting secrets, oh my, oh my!
Whisk it good, let's have some fun,
Creamy chaos for everyone.

In the fridge, a stick awaits,
Wink and smile, it elevates.
Spread your joy, don't be afraid,
Life's too short for bland charades.

Taste the salty, taste the sweet,
Find the rhythm, feel the beat.
Butter's dance on heated pan,
Wobbling like a goofy man.

Melt the edges, crisp the gold,
Funny stories still untold.
Joy's a recipe to explore,
Spread it thick, there's always more.

A Taste of Mystique

In the oven, secrets hide,
Chocolate chips won't let it slide.
Mystique lingers, warm and bright,
Cookies laughing in their flight.

Doughy wonders on my tongue,
Every bite feels like I'm young.
Sugar chaos, wild and free,
Flavors dance, just wait and see!

Vanilla echoes in the air,
Sprinkled giggles everywhere.
A smidgen more, a wink of fate,
Whisked together, it feels great!

Mystery stirs in what we taste,
Joy's the batter, never waste.
Let's indulge in each delight,
Laugh with cookies through the night.

The Alchemy of Dough

Mixing magic, flour flies,
Dough transforms before my eyes.
Add some whimsy, fold it in,
Laughter bubbles, let's begin!

Oven's heat, a warm embrace,
Funny faces, cookie race.
Shape it round, or twist a bit,
Find the joy in every hit.

A dash of spice, a pinch of glee,
Every scoop feels wild and free.
Bake it thick, let dreams expand,
Share with friends, the best of plans.

A sprinkle here, a giggle there,
Doughy wonders fill the air.
In each bite, a story flows,
Life's sweet fun in cookie dough.

Doughy Dilemmas

In the bowl, a swirl of fate,
Chocolate chips and dreams await.
Do I bake it or just eat?
That's a question, oh so sweet!

Flour flying through the air,
Sticky fingers everywhere.
The recipe's a mystery,
But what's a life without some history?

Oven preheating, hearts alive,
Will these cookies help me thrive?
Mixing metaphors and dough,
Life's a treat, let's make it flow!

With every scoop, a giggle erupts,
Surprises waiting, life interrupts.
Shall I share or stash away?
Doughy dilemmas rule the day!

Fables Folded in Flour

Once upon a whisking dream,
A tale as rich as vanilla cream.
Sugar mountains, butter streams,
Life is sweeter than it seems!

In the cupboard, spices hide,
With a pinch of luck on my side.
Shall I dare to bake a pie?
Or munch the dough and let time fly?

Rolling pins and laughter blend,
In this kitchen, joy won't end.
Pursuing flavors with delight,
In fables folded, all is right!

Mixing stories, stirring fun,
Baking 'til the day is done.
Flour dust and wild swirls,
In this world, a joy unfurls!

The Heart's Ingredients

In a bowl, I find my soul,
A dash of hope, a sprinkle whole.
Eggs of laughter, whisked anew,
Finding joy in what I brew.

Salt of life, a pinch of strife,
Mix it in, that's how's my life.
A recipe for the heart,
With love added, it's pure art!

Rolling dough with hopeful hands,
Searching for sweet, not bitter lands.
I knead my dreams; they rise and grow,
In every batch, the love will show!

Bake it up, let it shine,
In the chaos, I find the rhyme.
The heart's ingredients, pure and bright,
In culinary joy, I take flight!

Searching for the Sweet Spot

In a cookie jar, I seek the best,
Crispy edges, soft inside, a test.
What's the secret? Whisk and pour?
Chasing sweetness, wanting more!

Oh, the joy of that doughy ball,
Will it rise or will it fall?
Every bite, a playful quest,
In every morsel, I'm so blessed!

A sprinkle here, a drizzle there,
Taste-testing with great flair.
Finding the spot that makes me cheer,
In cookie land, there's nothing to fear!

With giggles shared and flour fights,
Chasing flavors, reaching heights.
Searching for the sweet delight,
In every crumb, life feels just right!

The Essence of Unbaked Aspirations

In a bowl of dreams, I stir and swirl,
A sprinkle of laughter, a dash of twirl.
Chocolate chips glint, like hopes in the night,
But raw is the flavor, and oh, what a sight!

Eggs crack like secrets, flour flies high,
Whisking up wishes that wobble and sigh.
The taste of tomorrow's potential is sweet,
Yet all I can manage is dough on my feet!

Baking's a journey, where chaos can reign,
Mixing up troubles, once joy, now a pain.
Yet I laugh through the mess, with frosting on cheek,
Embracing the goofiness, leading the freak!

So here's to the dough, my muse and my jam,
For who needs perfection when you've got a plan?
I'll savor this batter, my dreams still aglow,
The essence of life in this clump of cookie dough!

Layers of Longing

I dream of a cake, but settle for dough,
Layers of longing, in an unbaked show.
Each scoop a wish, that doesn't quite rise,
A twist of the whisk, beneath sugary skies!

Chocolate and nuts in a sticky embrace,
Fate's baking humor leaves crumbs in my face.
But laughter's the icing that sweetens the plight,
As I pile up my dreams, just hoping for light!

A sprinkle of joy in the mixture swirls round,
Reality's crunch, what a strange sound!
Yet in every lump, a smile takes form,
For this lumpy adventure is my morning norm!

So here's to the layers of crumbs that we bake,
With each humorous mishap, our spirits shall wake.
For while life's recipe might get oddly gooey,
The joy in the mixing is what makes it truly!

Recipe for the Soul's Palette

In a kitchen of chaos, I gather my tools,
A pinch of ambition, but who really rules?
Sugar spills out, like secrets gone wide,
The recipe's lost, but I'm along for the ride!

Baking soda dreams, rising high with a pop,
My hopes bounce around, like eggs that won't drop.
Flour in the air, a sneeze turns to glee,
As the soul's palette dances, so wild and so free!

Not measured, not mixed, like my thoughts in the mix,
Ovens may bake, but I'm savoring tricks.
Laughter's the whisk that blends fun with the mess,
Until life gives me cookies—I'm feeling so blessed!

So gather 'round friends, let's bake with delight,
In the warmth of the kitchen, we'll share our insight.
Forget all the rules, let the flavors align,
In this recipe wild, our hearts brightly shine!

The Dough of Discovery

In the bowl of existence, I knead with my hands,
Squishing my worries, ignoring the plans.
Flavors of confusion, a sprinkle of bliss,
The dough of discovery, sealed with a kiss!

Each stir tells a story, each roll is a whim,
A sprinkle of madness on the edge of a brim.
The future's a cookie, still soft in the middle,
While I laugh through the mess and embrace every riddle!

So let's toss in some giggles, a dose of delight,
For life's just a party, wrapped snugly in white.
A pinch of aspirations and a generous dash,
Until all of my dreams come alive with a splash!

So here's to the dough, our timeless refrain,
With humor as yeast, we'll rise once again.
Through the mix-up and mayhem, our spirits will soar,
In this dough of discovery, we always want more!

Insights from the Mixing Bowl

In a bowl of fluff and cream,
I ponder life, or so it seems.
With eggs and sugar, a dance begins,
What joy is hidden in these spins?

Choco chips fall with a plop,
Dreams of cookies, I can't stop.
Do they hold the secrets, oh so grand?
Or just crumbs in a floury land?

Roll it out, give it a shove,
Each scoop is filled with endless love.
A sprinkle here, a dash of flair,
What wisdom hides, if I dare?

Yet taste reveals the sweetest fate,
A recipe born from blissful state.
For in each bite, a giggle rolls,
Mysteries lie beneath our doughy souls.

Beyond Sweet Sensations

Mixing flour with thoughts in tow,
Sweet dreams rise, then fade like snow.
Baking powder sparks, oh what fun,
Are treats the answer or just a pun?

With vanilla whispers in the air,
I laugh at life, without a care.
Sprinkled secrets in every swirl,
What truths unfurl in this sweet whirl?

Is there a lesson, hidden in cream?
Like life, it flows, or so it may seem.
Stirring chaos with a wink so bright,
I embrace the taste of silly delight.

Oven's warmth wraps me like a hug,
As batch after batch gives me a tug.
In cookie forms, I find my cheer,
Life's strange recipe is crystal clear!

A Quest in Each Layer

A quest unfolds with each new mix,
In gooey bliss, I scramble and fix.
What's in this bowl, a dream or a dare?
Each bite taken, a flavor to share.

Layered hopes in sweet delight,
Creamy fantasies take flight.
The purpose hides in sprinkles bright,
Ha! It's just dough, but what a sight!

Rolling pin and laughter collide,
Through twists and turns, I slide and glide.
Does fortune lie in melted charms?
Or just in glee and baking arms?

A batch of wisdom, slightly raw,
In cookie dough, I find my flaw.
Yet joy abounds, and oh, the cheer,
In frosted moments, meaning's near!

From Batter to Belief

Flour clouds have me lost in dreams,
An epic tale in butter streams.
Whisk in questions, layer in cheer,
Sweet surprises are always near.

A pinch of salt, just for good luck,
Laughter bubbles, we're both struck.
Do colors hold the answers true?
Or just paint a scene, a whimsical view?

Scoop by scoop, life's challenges rise,
With chocolate chunks, I touch the skies.
Fatigued yet sweet, I find my core,
In every bite, there's something more.

Baked for moments, crisp and bright,
From batter to belief, I take flight.
And so I giggle, at my own little quest,
For in cookie dough, I'm truly blessed.

Crumbs of Contemplation

In a bowl of dough, I ponder and stir,
What lies within? A grand thought or a blur?
Chocolate chips beckon, like treasures concealed,
Mixed with floury dreams, they slowly revealed.

Tiny bites of wisdom, I roll into balls,
Each one a question, or maybe just halls
Of sweetness and sprinkles, oh what a delight,
Unraveling secrets, like stars in the night.

Sifting through sugar, I find my delight,
In crumbs of the past, both wrong and quite right.
The oven will bake them to crispy brown gold,
Yet the best of the answers? Just nibble, be bold!

Kitchen philosopher, I check on my fate,
With a sprinkle of joy, I just can't wait!
The dough's all around me, a soft, warm embrace,
And like my life's questions, it's all a big chase.

Sweet Unraveling

Bowls and spoons gather, what chaos will thrive?
Creamy sweet madness, keeps hopes alive.
Fingers deep in dough, where flavors collide,
I wonder if nonsense is where truths reside.

What's life without chocolate? A riddle, I bet!
I'll dip in the batter, and plunge without fret.
Morsels of laughter sprinkles my day,
As I whisk up my dreams in this sugary fray.

My apron's a canvas, a palette of fun,
Creating a masterpiece, one scoop at a run.
With each bite of joy, I submit to the fate,
Of cookie dough wonders; it's never too late!

I pause for a moment, each taste a surprise,
In gooey reflections, I find where joy lies.
The oven timer dings, a sweet serenade,
As I dive into laughter, in this life I've made.

In the Heart of Batter

In the heart of the batter, I'm lost in a trance,
A sprinkle of chaos, a dash of romance.
Eggs cracked with wisdom, flour clouds of thought,
Each blob a reminder of lessons I sought.

With a flick of the wrist, dilemmas take flight,
As I fold in the joy that makes days feel right.
Rolling in sweetness, I giggle and jest,
These clumps of reflection, oh they're simply the best!

Baking's a journey, with crispy detours,
Spoons serve as guides through the gooey outdoors.
A brown sugar guardian, so clever and sly,
Reminds me of dreams that sometimes run high.

So here's to the batter, the mess and the fun,
Each scoop carries laughter, till baking is done.
With cookies around me, my heart surely sings,
For meaning in desserts, oh the joy that it brings!

Whispers of Vanilla Essence

In a swirl of soft whispers, vanilla's embrace,
I dip into mystery, this endless race.
A scent filled with laughter, it dances in air,
I find bits of wisdom, in crumbs here and there.

Stirring the dreams with a generous hand,
Batter and giggles form a playful band.
What's next in this mixing? A tasty delight,
As I ponder life's questions, beneath kitchen light.

Laughter bakes slowly, in nature's sweet glow,
A pinch of the nutty, helps insight to flow.
Each dollop a lesson, each sprinkle a laugh,
In the bowl of existence, I carve out my path.

When time rolls around for those cookies to feast,
A riddle well baked, my joy's been released.
The essence of sweetness, brings meaning anew,
In the laughter of batter, I find what is true.

A Dash of Introspection

In the bowl of life, we stir and bake,
Mixing hopes and dreams, for goodness sake.
With every scoop, we taste and try,
Finding the sprinkles beneath the pie.

Flour on my face, I sift through doubt,
Wondering what life's really about.
Is it sugar or spice that gives us glee?
Or the half-eaten bites, just meant for me?

I knead my thoughts, like dough so sweet,
Rolling through laughter, with sticky feet.
If the oven's hot, will I rise on cue?
Or burn myself silly, like cookies do?

Baked or raw, it's all the same,
I dip in sweetness, not for the fame.
In crumbs I find the giggles tucked,
In life's recipe, I'm joyously stuck.

The Hidden Recipe of Life

A pinch of chaos, a drop of joy,
Mix it together, oh boy, oh boy!
In every swirl, the secrets hide,
Like chocolate chips, broad and wide.

I whisk my worries, stir my delight,
With each flick of the wrist, it feels just right.
Is it eggs or cream that holds the key?
Or the laughter shared, just to be free?

Bake until golden, but not too long,
In the crazy kitchen, where we belong.
Burnt edges, I laugh at the feeble crack,
For life's crazy taste, I'll never go back.

So I roll the dough, and let it chill,
Finding flavors that fit like a thrill.
In each gooey bite, a lesson may show,
Life's hidden recipe, let it flow.

Luscious Layers of Understanding

In layers of dough, so thick and grand,
Each roll we make, with a little hand.
Chocolate chunks, our deeper thoughts,
Frosting dreams, that can't be bought.

I split the batter, see the divide,
Between the goo and the crumbly side.
What feels like chaos, may just be art,
Like mismatched cookies that warm the heart.

Sprinkle some laughter, and bake a while,
In this funny kitchen, let's dance and smile.
For every bite, there's a tale to tell,
Like flour clouds that make us swell.

So grab a spoon, let's dig around,
In creamy delights, our joy is found.
In outrageous flavors, we twist and blend,
Finding answers in snacks, around the bend.

Cookie Crumbs and Cosmic Questions

With cookie crumbs scattered near and far,
I'm munching on thoughts, like a candy bar.
What makes a cookie both soft and crispy?
Why can't life's riddles be less frisky?

I sprinkle my doubts, let them rise high,
While the oven hums, like a wise old guy.
The taste of existence can be quite a plot,
Like a cookie dough mystery, piping hot.

Should I add more chocolate? Or just embrace?
The sweet, sweet chaos of life's funny race.
With every bite, I contemplate fate,
Craving wisdom while snatching a plate.

In the dough of creation, we mix and mold,
Cosmic questions in the oven unfold.
So let's crumble and crumble, we'll never pout,
For cookie crumbs hold the answers, no doubt!

www.ingramcontent.com/pod-product-compliance
Lightning Source LLC
Chambersburg PA
CBHW051658160426
43209CB00004B/940